zen

meditations

on being a true friend

richard craze

zen
meditations
on being a true friend

SOURCEBOOKS, INC.®
NAPERVILLE, ILLINOIS

Without friends we are alone in the world. A friend is someone with whom we can be ourselves, whom we can share with and laugh with, and whom we can turn to when the world grows cold.

Friendship sweetens life, it makes the good times better, and the bad times easier to bear. And yet it is all too easy to take a friend for granted, to fail to realize what we have until we lose it. Friendship is a gift, but not one that should be treated lightly, it must be treasured, looked after, endlessly renewed and nurtured.

This little book of meditations celebrates the joy of friendship, and provides the perfect opportunity to spend a little time thinking about friends, past and present. It encourages contemplation and appreciation of friendship, in a world which is often too busy and hectic to allow quiet thought. To accompany the meditations there is a CD of music which has been specially composed to reflect the varied moods of friendship and to ease contemplation. Take a few minutes out of your day to dwell on some of the meditations, and through this time thinking about the value of friendship, you will find the energy to strengthen and regenerate those relationships that are important to you. The music can be used in conjunction with the meditations, or alone as a tool to aid relaxation.

the call of a friend

I had friends. They called to me in the silence of my heart. I heard their summons, their note of distress, even in the clamor of the world and I went to them. I asked no questions beyond "how can I help." I gave no judgment. The duty of friendship is to give help, to lend a hand, to provide support and nurture when the call comes.

I had friends. They called to me in the silence of my heart.

A very long time ago in Japan there were two friends. One played a stringed instrument and the other listened. They both performed their role equally skillfully. When the musician played a tune about mountains or water the listener would say, "I can see mountains," or, "I can hear the running water."
The listener grew old and died, and the musician cut the strings of his instrument— never to play again. Since then the cutting of strings has always been a Zen sign of intimate friendship.

true friends

choice of friends

Friendship isn't like going to the library and borrowing a novel on a casual basis. Friendship is more like nurturing and caring for an old book; dusting it off; rereading it with love and care. We may know the story, the order of the words, the chapter titles, and even the ending, but we still derive enormous pleasure from the way the book is put together. So it is with friendship. We know our friends' gestures and responses, expressions and moods, but we still derive satisfaction from being in their company time and time again.

A true friend is like a very rare and valuable book.

you are

The world turned its back on me but you didn't.

The world thought me a fool but you didn't.

The world laughed at me, you didn't.

my friend

When everyone else walked out you walked in. When everyone else deserted me you were there to pick me up. When everything was dark and unbending you were there with light and comfort. When I thought I had reached the end of the road you urged me on another mile. When there was no hope you brought it. When there was confusion you brought clarity. And when there were good times again you were there to share them with me. You are my friend.

by
my
side

I don't need a leader to
follow. I don't need a
follower to trail in my
footsteps. I don't need a
support or a crutch. I
don't need a victim or
someone to rescue. I need
a friend to walk by my
side and be a companion.

what is a friend?

A friend is someone who comes when you need them.

When you are ill they plump up your pillows, make tea, bring flowers, and let you talk until you feel sleepy. And then they quietly slip away without waking you to say good-bye.

remembering
good friends

I count myself in nothing else so happy

When we look back, will it be the money we have made and spent that we remember? The loves won and lost? Or the good friends that we have made and still have by us? Good friends love us unconditionally and cannot be frittered away like money. Good friends won't desert us for another lover, friendship is not exclusive, it can be shared and, in doing so, grows in our love.

As in a soul remembering my good friends

Richard II, William Shakespeare

Friendship is like a plant. In the early stages we have to water and nurture it. As it grows we take pleasure from its increasing strength. And when it finally comes to bloom, it repays all our endeavors and we delight in its colors, its fragrant scent, and its beauty. And friendship, like a flower, will have its seasons. When the petals of friendship drop away we know it is only a passing time, and come the spring it will return and we will welcome it back with renewed enthusiasm and love.

nurturing
friendships

I love everything that's old; old friends,
old times, old manners, old books, old wines.

She Stoops to Conquer, Oliver Goldsmith

old friends

A true friendship, like a fine wine, will only improve with age. It grows heady with taste, intoxicating with richness, and gains in value. But unlike a fine wine it cannot be completely emptied; no matter how much we drink of it, there is always more to pour. An old friendship is something to be savored, it doesn't go out of favor or fashion. It is one of the greatest riches of life.

There is

an old

Chinese

saying: Spend old money on new friends, new money on

old friends—and if you truly want to honor a friend

write their name on the wings of a dragon. If you

want to honor a friend then the idea of a dragon

on the wings of a

soaring in splendor with your friend's name written

on its wing is a fine and noble vision indeed. How

could you not want to honor your friends? How could

you achieve this in a dragonless age?

dragon

the smallness of friendship

Friendship is a small thing. It cannot be bought, sold, bartered or traded, it costs nothing. It cannot be manufactured, designed or updated. It cannot be measured or weighed, nor can its volume be found. It doesn't require you to fall in love as a relationship does, but it does contain an element of love. It doesn't require unending sacrifice as having a family does, but it contains elements of family within it. It can stand long periods apart and still be strong. It can suffer arguments and disagreements and still be enduring. It is a small thing, friendship, but the world would be much smaller without it.

a rejoicing
of friendship

When I fail, my friends cheer me up, dust me off and set me back on the path. They take no delight in my downfall as my enemies do. When I succeed they rejoice with me. They are not jealous. They do not temper my joy with criticism or advice. They are simply happy to share my triumphs without taking anything away from my moment. They never expect too much of me, and my failures make no difference to them. They give me support, help, comfort and, most importantly, are just there where I know they will be.

the
non-mask
of friendship

With my lover I have to wear a mask, we all do. We
strut, and pretend, and declare our love but never truly
reveal all of ourselves. We all do this and it is necessary
to maintain the illusion. But with my
friends I can strip away the mask
and be myself. I have nothing
to gain by pretending
anything, and they would
see through my attempts.

With
my friends
I can be the real me
I can dare to be
myself.

defining friendship

The word friend comes form the
Old English "frëond"
which means "free."

A friend is someone who
sets you free. Allows you
to be free. Gives you the
freedom and space to be
yourself. Doesn't hem you
in or impose restrictions. A
friend allows you to settle,
to be relaxed, and just to
be. A friend is the gateway
to freedom.

a friend is
someone
who lies
to you

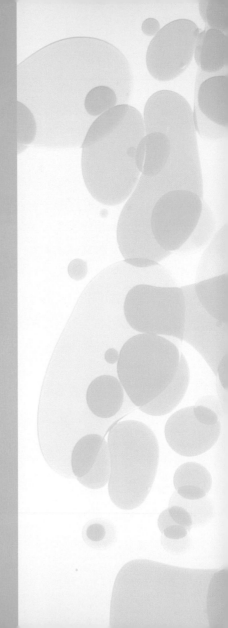

Thank heavens we have friends, for they are the ones who will lie to us. When they've seen our ex-lover they'll tell us how unhappy they looked. When we have failed they will tell us what a marvelous opportunity we've just created for growth and learning. When we wear something totally unsuitable they will tell us how good we look. When we need to lose weight they will tell us cuddly is in. They are the ones who tell us those little white lies no one else would dare to—and they are the ones we know are lying and we love them for it as it is done without malice or judgment.

Life is a bit of bread and butter. That's all we have. Some of us have a little less butter and some of us have stale bread. But we all have a little bit of bread and butter.

A friendship is something that puts a little bit of honey on the bread and butter of life. We can survive without it, but it certainly sweetens our way.

a little honey

filling in the silences

In all conversations there are silences

those little pauses where nothing gets said. In some conversations there is a need to fill those silences, to jump in with further gossip or chat. But a friendship is one place where those silences don't have to be filled. A friendship is somewhere where you can relax and allow that silence to speak volumes all of its own about the need for privacy and space and freedom. Somewhere where you are both content to take a breather from life and just sit and be; to enjoy each other's company without having to speak. Friendship fills the silence without words.

Imagine the world full of darkness. A lover can illuminate the gloom with brief flashes of joy, and the birth of a child is a steady beam of hope. A friend doesn't bring light but a hand to hold in the darkness for comfort. A friend isn't there to lead or guide you through the dark, but to walk by your side in equality and balance. A friend is there to share the darkness and not to offer advice or help about how to dispel the dim mystery of life.

A friend is there to walk with you in the darkness and stumble with you and to make you laugh at your fear of the dark.

a friend in the dark

reserved for friends

Your heart is big enough to hold many people— lovers, children, partners, parents, and family. But there is a special place within your heart that is reserved for a very few special friends. That space cannot be filled with anyone else. That space has a permanent "reserved" sign on it that cannot be moved aside to make room for anyone but close friends. And until that space is filled your heart will always seem half empty.

It is better to have one true friend than hundreds of acquaintances. Friendship takes time and care to develop, it needs nurturing and protecting. It is as difficult to have a huge number of "intimate friends" as it is to juggle with thirty balls and keep them all in the air at the same time.

one true friend

True happiness consists not in the multitude of friends, But in the worth and choice.

Ben Jonson

musical
friends

I see myself as a musical note. I vibrate like a stringed instrument. My friends also make a similar sound—but different from mine. Together we make music. When we play together we have a harmony. With different friends I play different music. There is no competition. Sometimes I like to play soft and slow, and at other times loud and fast. I need different friends for different concerts, to create different moods and music. My friends are my symphony, my chorus, my melody.

I have a friend. She turns up when she wants, never when she says she will. She is

I have a friend

unreliable,
late,
irresponsible,
embarrassing,
loud,
uncouth,
and wild.
I have a friend. I love her because
she is everything I yearn to be
and everything I dare not be.

the word

We have one word for love—love. We have to use
this word for the way we feel about our partner,
children, family, parents, and friends. But this word
has so many different meanings that when we say we

for love

love our friends we cannot
express exactly what we mean.
The word isn't big enough or
grand enough to cover what

we feel. We can say we love you in forgiveness, in
comfort, in acceptance, in sharing, and in joy.

The word love isn't enough
but it is all we have and
we need to say it more.

losing friends

To maintain our friendships we have to service them, make repairs, give them a lick of paint, have them regularly checked for faults and the beginnings of problems. We have to make an effort or they fall into disrepair. We have to be the first to cross the street.

In every friend we lose a part of ourselves, and the best part.

Alexander Pope, *Letters. 1714*

the best part of

friendship

It is true we lose a part of ourselves in every friend—but they also lose a part of themselves in us. It is an exchange, a mutual giving where they open their heart to us, and we to them. We can then give and take the best part and replace it with our own. By this collective replacement we both grow and improve until we are able to give to other friends—and so it goes on. Each giving and taking, each growing and expanding in love and affection.

the mathematics of friendship

Friendships have a curious mathematics all of their own. When we share our troubles with a friend they are miraculously halved, but our friend hasn't taken half of the burden. When we are celebrating, a friend will double our joy, but will not have to bring any along themselves. Friendships multiply our happiness and divide our sorrow. Friendships add something intangible but essential to our life. Without them our lives are lessened—there is something taken away that may have never even been there.

I no doubt deserved my enemies,
but I don't believe I deserved my friends.

"Song of Myself," Walt Whitman

the friends
we deserve

Our enemies are small and petty and deserved. But our friends are big and grand and wonderful. Do we deserve them? They would not be our friends if we did not. They are ours and we deserve them and they deserve us. Our enemies are not chosen, not cultivated, not nurtured and encouraged. They appear by default whereas our friends are chosen and invited, nursed and encouraged. We deserve them for the work we do.

Long after you have gone, I find myself still smiling, still chuckling over something you said. I find my mood lightened, lifted, and I feel glad you came and shared some time with me. Long after you've gone, I remember you and feel warmed and comforted.

long after you've

gone

thank you

I want to
thank you
for being
my friend. I want to sing your praises and
shout to everyone how utterly brilliant you are. I
want the world to know that having you as a friend
has enriched my life. Without you I would flounder
and lose my way, and I want you to know that I really
appreciate you being my friend and that I will repay
your generosity, faith, support, and kindness in the
only way I know how, by being your friend in return.

Thank you.

Friendship
is sharing. Not sharing our
things or our money, although we
may well do that as well. Friendship is
sharing those moments when we feel
delighted, awed, enthralled,
enchanted, and overwhelmed by sharing
the beauty of nature. What is
the point of seeing a beautiful sunset if you
don't have a friend there to share it with?
You don't have to say anything
—it's all in a look.

1

sharing

How much better is a rainbow if you have a friend there to point it out to! And the first daffodil of spring begs to be shared, as do the bluebells, the snowdrops, and the primroses. The fall bonfires are so much richer, so much more evocative when you have a friend with you. And the crispness of the first snows of winter definitely call out for a friend to be with you to run with, to throw snowballs with, to get cold with— and after to share hot chocolate with in front of a roaring log fire.

2

A very good meal is best eaten with good friends. If you take a business colleague to lunch you jockey for position and talk money and ideas. If you take a lover you flirt and hold hands. If you take your children you argue and discipline. But if you take a friend you savor the food; take pleasure in the company; relax and generally enjoy everything. A meal with a friend is to be lingered over, and remembered afterward with affection.

eating with friends

my

When I was small I believed in magic. As I grew older the magic vanished and I was left alone in the harsh, real world of grown-ups. Then my friend came along and did magic for me. He brought me light and hope and comfort. He eased my burden, picked me up when I was down,

friend the magician

increased my joy a thousandfold, stayed with me when I was afraid, worked miracles around me, showed me the true meaning of unconditional love and became my magician.

a friend is
like the
forces of
nature

When it's winter we have no evidence of the spring, yet we know it will return and bring new hope and joy. Friendship is like that. We don't have to have a set date when a friend will return; it is enough to know they are out there and will come back, bringing new hope and joy.

The forces of nature and friendship work the same, hidden at times, secret, powerful, and utterly reliable.

the value
of friendship

I can make enough money to buy anything I want, and I will be lonely. I can share my life with enough lovers that I will be completely satisfied, but I will still be lonely. I can travel the world and see all the fabulous sights, and I will still be lonely. I can converse with world leaders and politicians, and still be lonely. I can cavort with film stars and celebrities, and still be lonely. I can get one phone call from a friend and feel loved, complete, not lonely any more. That's what I value the most.

When I achieve my dreams,
my goals, my ambitions I am
bursting to tell my friend.

bursting to tell

When it has all gone wrong I simply have to
share my grief—but anyone will do. When life is
important and the big happy stuff happens
around me, I am simply bursting to tell a friend
because without them it all means nothing.

My mother always straightens my collar. My partner always tucks back that bit of stray hair I have that hangs down over my forehead. My children tell me what to wear when I pick them

friends don't tidy me

up from school so I won't embarrass them. But my friends don't tidy me up—that's why they are my friends. With them I can be me and be as untidy and embarrassing as I want and they still love and accept me for being me.

up

I told you so

My friend said not to, but I did. I went ahead and did it anyway and it all went wrong. And afterwards, when I was left to pick up the pieces, my friend comforted me, and the one thing I never heard was, "I told you so."

two cups

The spring has come now
But the wind is blowing cold
I still set two cups

When will you come back
For I miss you my old friend
I still set two cups

one true friend

When things are going well for you, when you have plenty of money, your health is good and life is smiling at you, then you will have no shortage of friends. It is only when the chips are down, when life looks bleak that you learn who your real friends are.

Fairweather friends are two a penny, one true friend is worth her weight in gold.

Friendship is a vast old tree. Each friend is a leaf that has its season, its time to be, and when that time is over it will curl and fade and fall from the tree. But the space left behind is only to be filled with another leaf just the same—but different. So our friends have their seasons, their time, and when it is over, when our relationship has run its course, then they too must be allowed to fall away gracefully and naturally. There will be others. There always are.

all my friends

the field

Friendship is a field. You have to prepare it, plough it, remove the weeds, plant good seed, watch over it, water it when it needs it, scare away the birds, check the weather, and nourish it. When the time is right you will be rewarded with a great harvest. If you fail to prepare the field well your seeds will fail and the weeds will grow, at harvest time there will be nothing to gather in to fill the barns of your heart.

friendships that

cannot be broken

Friendship is an iron chain. The more links we forge, the greater the strength of that chain. But it is only as strong as each link and we must forge each well and with infinite care. The chain may become stretched, used, worn, but it cannot be broken if the friendship was pounded on anvils of love.

city of friends

I dream'd in a dream I saw a
city invincible to the attacks
of the whole of the rest of
the earth,
I dream'd that was the new
city of Friends.

"I Dream'd in a Dream,"
Walt Whitman

still
remembering

Time has come and gone. Lots of
water has flowed but I still
remember you. Still hear your voice
in my mind in times of trouble. You
cannot be here now as you have
gone off on new adventures, new
journeys, but I still remember you as if
you were here yesterday. Such is our
friendship that death itself has not
broken our bond, not even rippled our
love. I am here and you are not, but it
is as if we are still friends, still
together. I am still remembering and I
believe you to be so as well.

the

beauty of friendship

The true beauty of friendship is not in calling on friends in times of trouble and need, but in knowing that we might call upon them if such times arise. Friends are like savings. We don't want to squander our hard-earned money on trivialities. Savings are for emergencies which we hope will never happen. True friendship is also for emergencies which we hope will never happen. The beauty of friendships is that we can save and count our savings and hopefully never have to spend them.

the
breath
of kindness

A friend is one to whom we
may pour out all the contents
of our heart, chaff and grain
together, knowing that the
gentlest of hands will take and
sift it, keep what is worth
keeping and with a breath of
kindness blow the rest away.

Arabian Proverb

multi-talented friends

Having friends is better than having to employ counselors, psychiatrists, healers, therapists, and psychologists. Friends are multi-talented and have all the skills needed to stop you going mad. They comfort you, nurture you, help you, listen to you, give you good advice, guide you, and every day drag you back from the brink. Your friends are your medicine, your process, your cure, your doctors, and your saviors.

sharing

A friend is there, not
just for the good times,
the times of celebration
and success, but for the
dark times, the times when
things go wrong, when life
seems bleak. That is the beauty
of friendship, that we must take
the joy and the sorrow in equal
weight, and that in turn, we know
we will always have someone to
share our laughter and our pain.

If the sun is our parents welcoming us into the world with light and warmth and encouragement; and the moon is our lover, emotional, mysterious, deep, then the rainbow is the symbol of our friends. The rainbow has no purpose, it doesn't feed or clothe us, it doesn't provide us with a family or love or support—and yet what a colorless, drear world this would be without the rainbow to brighten it up. It stands as a sign that we can have joy without reason, elation without incentive and optimism without motive.

The rainbow and friendships bring us a little joy, a little comfort, a little hope.

Some flowers grow tall while others don't; some streams gush while others trickle.

differences

If we love our friends for what they are, we will have to accept their way of doing things. Not everyone shares all of our own particular attitudes. Friends are often more valuable for their differences to us than for their similarities. We must accept our friends for themselves, just as we expect them to accept us.

freedom

Friendship is a freedom

A freedom to be who we really are. To say what we really mean. To explore ourselves without guise or having to remember tact or diplomacy. Friendship is the freedom to explore human relationships without the entanglement of sex or love, and it is the freedom to make ourselves of some use without having to volunteer—we will be called upon if necessary. The freedom of friendship is in how freely it is given.

Sourcebooks, Inc.
P.O. Box 4410, Naperville, Illinois 60567-4410
(630) 961-3900
FAX: (630) 961-2168

Text © Richard Craze 2000
Cover design: The Big Idea
Interior design: Susannah Good
Cover image: F. Cunningham, Flowers & Foliage
Interior images © Digital Vision
Series Editor: Elizabeth Carr

Printed in Italy

MQ 10 9 8 7 6 5 4 3 2 1

ISBN: 1-57071-645-5

Note on the CD

The music that accompanies this book has been specially commissioned from composer David Baird. Trained in music and drama in Wales, and on the staff of the Welsh National Opera & Drama company, David has composed many soundtracks for both the theater and radio.

The CD can be played quietly through headphones while relaxing or meditating on the text. Alternatively, lie on the floor between two speakers placed at equal distances from you. Try and center your thoughts, and allow the soundtrack to wash over you and strip away the distracting layers of the outside world.